Helping Your Child with Reading and Writing

INTRODUCTION

When children first come to school they have already learned a vast amount. They have learned how to go to the toilet, how to feed and dress themselves. They have learned all kinds of things about the world around them and, most importantly, they have learned to talk.

> **Parents Are Their Children's First And Best Teachers**

When children start school it is important that teachers can learn from parents about their children and that parents and teachers can work together in partnership to make sure that children's learning at school is as successful as it has been at home.

Many parents ask teachers what they can do at home to help. Here are some ideas of the things you can do to help your child become a reader and a writer. You will probably find that you already do them!

Think about how your child learned to talk . . . learning to read is a similar process. Children learn about reading by listening to stories, by making up a story as they turn the pages of the book and by reading print of all kinds.

Emily: asking questions about the writing all around when I was a baby

READING

What can I do at home to help my child read?

Read to your child, share books, share your enjoyment of stories.

If you have the time and if your child wants to, read together with your child. The pleasantest way for this to happen is for you and your child to sit close together somewhere comfortable and share a book or two, in the same way that you probably already share rhymes, songs or jingles.

Tom: reading to my little sister.
She'd rather watch telly!

You can also talk about print as you see it around you at home or in the street — the writing on the cornflake box, your child's name on a birthday card, the name of your street, the writing on television adverts, the details of television programmes.

It will help, too, if your child sees you reading. Young children like to copy their parents, so children will read if they see you reading — whatever you read . . . magazines, the newspaper, recipes, the *TV Times*, books.

Children learn best when they feel confident, so try to find something encouraging to say about your child's reading.

What do you mean by 'share a book'?

There are lots of ways you can share books. You can look at the pictures together and talk about them. As you are reading a story you can ask 'What do you think is going to happen next?' Gradually your child will begin to look more and more closely at the print.

Read to your child or make up stories. You can read one page and your child another.

What should I do if my child doesn't want to read?

If reading is fun, your child will want to share it with you. And, of course, if you have beautiful picture books to share, your child will enjoy them.

Raqib: my dad reading to me.

Whatever You Do Don't Force Your Child To Read

Make the time fun for both of you.

What should I do if my child gets stuck on a word?

There are two things you can do. The simplest thing is to say the word and let your child carry on with the story. Or you can ask the child to guess. And if the guess is a good one — if it still makes sense — then you should accept it.

Let's look at an example:
Your child is reading this sentence:

'You could ride your bicycle'

She gets stuck on the word 'bicycle'. If she says 'bike' or 'trike' or 'BMX' the meaning of the sentence is not changed.

Making Mistakes Is Part Of Learning To Read

What matters is that your child can make sense of what she is reading.

I worry when my child knows the story by heart but doesn't look at the words. What should I do?

Children learn lots of stories by heart and they practise reading by telling the story, at first without looking at the words. It is an important part of learning to read.

3

But from very early on, when sharing books with children, try to get them to 'engage' with the text so that they are hearing the story, getting the meaning, but also being drawn into getting involved in the reading process itself. So you can ask your child to 'read' particular bits — things like people's names or a repeating sequence like

'Not now, Bernard'

or

'Oh no!' said Mr Bear 'I can't stand this!'

Once children have had a lot of experience of doing this and of playing games with the words, you will find that they start, in the re-telling of the story, to get closer and closer to the real thing. You can play games and get your child to look more closely at words by finding words that look the same in the story, or words that start with the same letter as the child's name, or words that look the way they sound, like 'BUZZ' or 'SPLAT'.

Where do I get books and what sort of books should I choose?

Books are expensive, but most schools encourage children to borrow books from school, to look after them and to return them to school.

You can borrow books from your local library and the librarian will be able to advise you on books.

Monya: going to the library.

5

Many schools run bookshops where you can buy paperback books and bookshops in most of the large towns offer a good selection of books.

Books are sold nowadays in supermarkets and chain stores and you can buy your child story tapes, where the child can hear the story on tape while following it in a book.

Jumble sales often have children's books for sale cheaply.

Wherever you go for books, let your child choose. You will be surprised at how good children are at knowing what books you choose. Some of them will be books that they can read with ease, some will be too difficult and will be books for you to read to them.

And remember all the beautiful picture story books you can buy and borrow. You will be spoiled for choice!

Will my child suffer if we don't speak English at home?

No. You will be able to share books with your child, sometimes in English and sometimes in the language you speak at home. Let your child tell you the story in your language and talk together about the pictures. You can read books together in your home language and, nowadays, there are several books available in English and another language.

The important thing to remember is that, as long as children know that you are involved with their reading, they will make progress.

At what age can I stop reading aloud to my children?

Keep on reading aloud to your child as long as your child wants you to. After all, most adults still like listening to stories and jokes!

What if I can't read or don't have the time to read every day?

Children can read to and with lots of people — brothers and sisters, grandparents, friends and neighbours and, of course, to themselves.

Sometimes it is good for a child to read to a younger brother, sister, cousin or friend. The child who is doing the reading is in the powerful position of being like the parents or the teacher.

WRITING

When children first come to school they already know a lot about writing and a lot of this knowledge comes from the writing they see around them — things like adverts, comics, notes for the milkman, shopping lists and letters. As with reading, children are more likely to write if they see their parents writing.

How do I know if my child can write?

Very young children like to make marks on paper. Very often these marks mean something to the child and the child may tell you that it is writing. It is important to take this seriously and to accept it as writing. After all, children had to practise talking by babbling and perhaps they have to practise writing by scribbling.

Later on, of course, your child will include some recognisable letters in this 'writing' and these will probably include the letters of the child's name. Perhaps your child will even be able to 'read' this writing and tell you what it says. In all probability you will not be able to read the child's writing yet as early attempts at writing often ignore things like spaces between words. But as the child sees more and more writing and learns more about it, you will notice changes — perhaps spaces between words, or marks like * to stand for spaces. You may even find your child putting in question marks, exclamation marks or full stops.

Rummana: reading an invitation to a birthday party.

Is there a right way to teach my child letters?

No, and it doesn't matter what sort of letters you use. Some children first learn to write capitals and others lower case letters like these. Some children's early attempts at writing imitate 'joined-up' writing. And if you speak a language at home other than English you will want to teach your child to write the script or alphabet or ideograms you use.

How often should I write with my child?

If your child wants to write and you have the time, fine. However, if your child is reluctant, don't insist. When you are writing — perhaps your shopping list or a letter — you can talk to your child about what you are doing and perhaps your child will want to write a list or letter of her or his own.

What sort of writing should be done at home?

Often the main writing that children do at school is writing stories and that is, of course, an important part of becoming a writer. However, you know that children do all sorts of other writing at home and you should try to encourage your child to do more. You will know that children like to write notices (MY ROOM, KEEP OUT), play schools with registers, help make shopping lists, leave messages, write thank you letters and birthday invitations, send off for free offers, write diaries, make up stories and plays, or play at post offices.

It is all writing and it is all valuable.

What about spelling?

Many children start off by inventing their own spellings. And, as with learning to talk and to read, making mistakes is part of learning to write. At first they may only get the first letter of the word more or less correct; then, perhaps, the first and last letter. But as they write more and more and have contact with books and stories they begin to know more and more about spelling.

Spelling is a bit like reading an unknown word. If your child is writing and asks how to spell a word, you could encourage the child to guess how to spell it, but if the child doesn't want to, just spell out the word. You might want to find out if your child's school uses letter names or the sounds of the letters and then do the same thing at home.

Nowadays many families have typewriters and computers at home and many children love playing with them. Encourage your child to write with them and perhaps make books of her or his own to read. In fact, if you have a computer at home, your child will benefit a lot more from having word-processing programmes to play with than from many of the so-called 'educational' programmes that are produced.

Sandra Smidt, Gillian Lathey, Gail Bedford
NATE 0–11 COMMITTEE AND WORKING PARTY 1988

SOME SUGGESTIONS OF BOOKS TO READ TO
AND WITH YOUR CHILD

Picture/Story Books in English

Ahlberg, Janet and Allan

The Baby's Catalogue	Picture Puffin
Burglar Bill	Picture Lions
Each Peach, Pear, Plum	Picture Lions
Funnybones	Picture Lions
Peepo!	Picture Puffin
The Jolly Postman	Heinemann

Baum, Louis

Are We Nearly There?	Bodley Head

Briggs, Raymond

The Snowman	Picture Puffin
Father Christmas	Picture Puffin

Browne, Anthony

Bear Hunt	Hippo

Burningham, John

Mr. Gumpy's Outing	Picture Puffin
Mr. Gumpy's Motor Car	Picture Puffin
Come Away From The Water, Shirley	Picture Lions
The Shopping Basket	Picture Lions
Would You Rather...	Picture Lions
Avocado Baby	Jonathan Cape
Where's Julius	Jonathan Cape

Carle, Eric

The Very Hungry Caterpillar	Picture Puffin

Cole, Babette

The Trouble With Mum	Picture Lions

Counsel, June

But Martin	Picture Corgi

Daly, Niki

Joseph's Other Red Sock	Picture Lions

Dickinson, Mary

Alex and Roy	Hippo
(and others in the same series)	

Gag, Wanda

Millions of Cats	Picture Puffin

Graham, Bob

Pete and Roland	Picture Lions

Hill, Eric

Where's Spot	Picture Puffin
(and other Spot books)	

Hughes, Shirley
    Alfie Gets In First   Picture Lions
    Alfie's Feet   Picture Lions
    Dogger   Picture Lions
    Chips and Jessie   Bodley Head

Hutchins, Pat
    Don't Forget the Bacon   Picture Puffin
    Goodnight Owl   Picture Puffin
    Happy Birthday, Sam   Picture Puffin
    Rosie's Walk   Picture Puffin
    Titch   Picture Puffin
    You'll Soon Grow Into Them, Titch   Picture Puffin

Isadora, Rachel
    My Ballet Class   Picture Lions

Kerr, Judith
    The Tiger Who Came To Tea   Picture Lions

Lobel, Arnold
    Frog and Toad Books   I Can Read

Mahy, Margaret
    The Boy Who Was Followed Home   Magnet

McKee, David
    Not Now, Bernard   Sparrow
    Tusk, Tusk   Sparrow

McPhail, David
    The Bear's Toothache   Magnet
    Where Can an Elephant Hide?   Magnet

Nicoll, Helen and Pienkowski, Jan
    Meg and Mog   Picture Puffin
    (and others about Meg and her cat Mog)

Offen, Hilda
    Rita the Rescuer   Magnet

Ormerod, Jan
    Be Brave, Billy   Picture Lions
    Sunshine   Picture Puffin
    Moonlight   Picture Puffin

Palin, Michael
    Small Harry and the Toothache Pills   Magnet

Parker, Christine
    Rebekah and the Slide   Dinosaur

Paul, Antony and Foreman, Michael
    The Tiger Who Lost His Stripes   Sparrow

Prater, John
    On Friday Something Funny Happened   Picture Puffin

Rose, Gerald
    Ahhh! Said Stork   Picturemac

Storytellers Series
The Raja's Big Ears *by Niru Desai*
(Thames Schools Television, February 1989)
The Enchanted Palace *by Ashim Bhattacharya
and Champaka Basu (Smarties Prize runner-up)*
The Golden Apple Tree *by Pervin Ulug*
The Hare and the Tortoise *by Gabriel Douloubakas*
Mitthu the Parrot *by Susheila Stone*
(video available from the Grosvenor Video Project)
The Naughty Mouse *by Susheila Stone*
(to be televised in 1989)
The Proud Elephant *by Qamar Zamani*
The Radish Thief *by Khodeja Khan*
Rona in the Moon *by Peter McLean*
To Heaven and Back *by Manohar Rakhe*

*All these titles are accompanied by audio
cassettes in Bengali, Gujarati, Punjabi
and Urdu*

Jennie Ingham Associates

Storytellers Series
The Wishing Tree *by Usha Bahl*
Ramu and the Tiger *by Susheila Stone*
The Moon Hare *by Susheila Stone*
King Jahangir and the Baby *by Indu Anand*
The Obstinate Hodja *by Kemal Sakarya*
(Thames Schools Television, February 1989)
King Akbar and the Poor Brahmin *by
Champaka Basu*

**Andre Deutsch with
Jennie Ingham Associates**

Tell Me a Tale Series
The Narrow Escape *by Qamar Zamani*
Exams! Exams! *by Usha Bahl*
The Sledge *by Barry Hancock*
The Pond that Disappeared *by Roy Smith*

*All these titles are accompanied by audio
cassettes in Bengali, Gujarati, Punjabi
and Urdu*

Thomas Nelson

Please send your orders to:
NATE Office
Birley School Annexe
Fox Lane
Frecheville
Sheffield S12 4WY

Helping Your Child with Reading and Writing

Bengali, Gujarati, Punjabi or Urdu at £3.50 for 5 copies; £30 for 50 copies.
English at £4.00 for 10 copies; £35 for 100 copies.

ISBN 0 901291 11 0